聰明的園丁 下

Wisdom from the Word

發現比喻的奧祕

作者‧洪善美 / 繪者‧青色、樹木、朴知賢

國家圖書館出版品預行編目 (CIP) 資料

聰明的園丁：發現比喻的奧祕 / 洪善美作；李明先
等繪 . -- 初版 . -- 臺北市：時兆，2018.09
　　冊；　公分
ISBN 978-986-6314-80-3(全套：精裝)

1. 聖經故事　2. 比喻

241.68　　　　　　　　　　　　　　107010673

作者｜洪善美
繪者｜李明先、林智勇、莫卡

董事長｜金時英
發行人｜周英弼
出版者｜時兆出版社
服務專線｜886-2-27726420
傳真｜886-2-27401448
地址｜台北市10556八德路二段410巷5弄1號2樓
網址｜www.stpa.org
電子信箱｜stpa@ms22.hinet.net

主編｜周麗娟
責任編輯｜由鈺涵
校對｜林思慧、陳美如
封面設計｜邵信成
內頁設計｜邵信成、李宛青
法律顧問｜宏鑑律師事務所　電話 886-2-27150270

商業書店總經銷｜聯合發行股份有限公司 TEL: 886-2-29178022
基督教書房｜基石音樂有限公司 TEL: 886-2-29625951
網路商店｜store.pchome.com.tw/stpa

ISBN｜978-986-6314-80-3（全套：精裝）
定價｜新台幣1200元（上下冊不拆售）
出版日期｜2018年9月 初版一刷

Original Korean & English edition copyright©2018 by Korean Publishing House

www.stpa.org

請掃 QR code
進入時兆官網
點選左側「免費會員專區」
填寫資料加入會員後
再點選左側「影音專區」
即可線上聽故事

聰明的園丁 下
Wisdom from the Word
發現比喻的奧祕

「當然！對爸爸來說，
妳是最棒的！但是比起這些
事，爸爸更喜歡妳是個內心溫暖
又誠實的人。」

"Of course! To me, you are the best!
But I like your warmth and honesty
more than your abilities."

「爸爸，我每件事都做
的比其他同學還要好哦！
爸爸，我最棒了，對吧？」

"Daddy! I think I am better than
my friends in everything.
Daddy! I am the best, right?"

法利賽人和稅吏
The Pharisee and the Publican

耶穌向那些仗著自己是義人，藐視別人的，設一個比喻，

說：「有兩個人上殿裡去禱告：一個是法利賽人，一個是稅吏。

法利賽人站著，自言自語地禱告說：『上帝啊，我感謝祢，我不像別人勒索、不義、姦淫，也不像這個稅吏。

我一個禮拜禁食兩次，凡我所得的都捐上十分之一。』

那稅吏遠遠地站著，連舉目望天也不敢，只捶著胸說：『上帝啊，開恩可憐我這個罪人！』

我告訴你們，這人回家去比那人倒算為義了；因為，凡自高的，必降為卑；自卑的，必升為高。」

（路加福音18：9－14）

嘰嘰……喳喳……嘰嘰……喳喳！
嘈雜的吵鬧聲不斷傳來，
只見許多人排在又彎又長的隊伍中，想要進入聖殿裡。

其中有留著大鬍鬚的大叔；
有牽著媽媽的手、蹦蹦跳跳的小孩；
有柱著柺杖的老爺爺、老奶奶和瘸腿的少年。
今天是在聖殿祈禱的日子。

Buzz…buzz…
There came noisy sounds.
Many people lined up to go into the synagogue.

Among them, there was an old man with a bushy beard,
a little boy holding his mom jumping up and down,
an old couple with a cane, and a crippled youth.
Today was the day of prayer at the synagogue.

但其中有一位特別顯眼的人。
他穿著華麗的衣服，衣角隨風飄逸，
他像國王一樣的走向聖殿。
「咳！咳！」他咳了兩聲。
蹬……蹬……蹬……他邁開大步走著，
所有人看到他，就都恭敬地低下頭，並往後退了一步
原來那是一個地位崇高的法利賽人，
他驕傲地把頭抬得高高的，
甚至連其他人看都不看一眼。

But there was one man catching everyone's attention.
With his splendid robe fluttering in the wind,
he walked into the synagogue like a king.
"Ahem!", He coughed. Stomp-stomp-stomp. He strode confidently.
All the people around him bowed and took a step backward.
He was a Pharisee who was in a high social standing.
The Pharisee proudly lifted his head high
and didn't even bother to look around.

9

另外有一個人卻儘可能地把自己藏起來，
不讓別人發現，那人就是收稅金的稅吏。
「如果我在這裡被人認出來的話，
可能會被別人用石頭打死的。」
因為稅吏常常多收很多稅金，又為難別人，
所以人們非常討厭他。
稅吏對於自己錯誤的行為感到很羞愧。

And there was another man
who was trying to hide himself from being found.
He was a publican.
"If they know who I am, I might be stoned to death."
He often harassed people and collected many taxes,
so people hated him.
The publican was aware of his fault, so he was ashamed of himself.

到達聖殿的時候，法利賽人用引人注意的聲音大聲地禱告。
「上帝啊！感謝祢！我不像那仗勢欺人的稅吏一樣，
我每週都規規矩矩的禁食禱告和奉獻十分之一。」
法利賽人還把自己做過的好事，一件件的說了出來。
人們都以尊敬的眼神看著他，但是上帝什麼話都沒有說。

When people arrived at the synagogue, they heard the Pharisee praying aloud.
"Lord, thank you! I am not like a publican who bullies people all the time.
I follow the rules and fast every week, and I always give you a tithe."
He listed all the great things that he had done.
All the people there looked at him in awe,
but God did not say anything.

稅吏默默地退到角落邊跪在那裡，
不讓人們聽到，低下頭來小小聲喃喃地禱告。

「上帝啊！請憐憫我，請饒恕我的過錯！
我願意把多收的稅金還給人，也不再為難他們了。」

稅吏發自內心的認錯悔改。
人們雖然仍在指責他，但上帝卻樂意饒恕他。

The publican knelt down in a corner with his head bowed
and prayed in such a quiet voice that nobody could hear him.

"Lord, be merciful! Please forgive me!
I will pay people back and will not bully them anymore."

He asked for forgiveness with all his heart.
People still condemned him, but God forgave him willingly.

15

「爸爸，我長得很高吧！
在朋友中我的個子是最高的。」

"Daddy! I grew a lot!
I am the tallest among my friends."

「真的嗎？妳真的長很高了！
當妳在媽媽的肚子裡時，
還像種子一樣小呢！」

"Oh yeah? You did grow a lot!
But when you used to be in your mommy's
tummy, you were as small as a seed!"

芥菜種
The Mustard Seed

祂又設個比喻對他們說：「天國好像一粒芥菜種，有人拿去種在田裡。
這原是百種裡最小的，等到長起來，卻比各樣的菜都大，且成了樹，天上的飛鳥來宿在它的枝上。」
（馬太福音13：31－32）

咚！
一粒芥菜種掉進了土裡。
「咦？好像有什麼東西掉下來了？」
咕溜……咕溜……
「啊！原來是你！
哇！你真是一個小不點的種子！」
土地給芥菜種一個溫暖地擁抱。

18

Dong!
A mustard seed fell on the ground.
"Huh? I thought I felt something falling on me?"
Wiggle, wiggle.
"Ha! It's you!
Wow, you are one small seed!"
The ground embraced the seed warmly.

19

芥菜種環顧了四周，發現有黑麥、芝麻、大豆、玉米和南瓜的種子。
芥菜種躡手躡腳地走到黑麥種子的旁邊。
「嘿！芝麻種子，你別動來動去。你弄得我好癢呀！」
「我？我沒有動啊！」
「蛤？那個動來動去的小不點兒是誰？是你嗎？」
「嘿！你也算是一顆種子嗎？哈哈哈！」
所有的種子都哈哈大笑起來。

The mustard seed looked around
and found a rye seed, a sesame seed, a bean, a corn seed, and a pumpkin seed.
Squirming, the mustard seed settled down beside the rye seed.
"Hey, Mr. Sesame seed, stop moving. It's so ticklish!"
"Me? I didn't even move."
"Huh? Then who was the little moving thing? Was it you?"
"Hey, are you a seed, too? Hahaha!"
Everyone laughed at the mustard seed.

「喂，小不點兒，你知道怎麼發芽長大嗎？」
芝麻種子驕傲地問道。
「就算他會發芽又怎樣？反正他也結不出多少果實！哈哈哈！」
大種子們不斷地取笑它，
但是芥菜種只是閉著眼睛，安靜地不說話。

"Hey, little one, can you even sprout?"
The sesame seed asked with pride.
"Even if he does, he won't be able to bear many fruits! Hahaha!"
The big seeds kept making fun of him,
but the mustard seed kept quiet and ignored the mocking.

鑽一鑽！扭一扭！種子們開始發芽了。
芥菜種也長出小小的芽。
大家都爭先恐後地長大，就好像在比賽一樣。
芥菜種比其他的種子更加努力地長大。

Wiggle-wiggle! All the seeds started to sprout.
The mustard seed also sprouted.
Everybody grew really fast as if they were in a competition.
The mustard seed made more effort than anyone else.

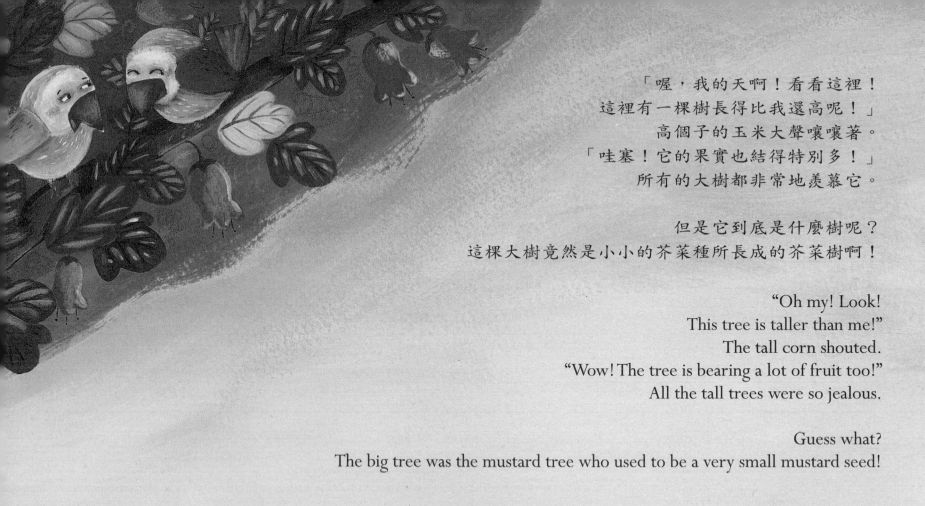

「喔，我的天啊！看看這裡！
這裡有一棵樹長得比我還高呢！」
高個子的玉米大聲嚷嚷著。
「哇塞！它的果實也結得特別多！」
所有的大樹都非常地羨慕它。

但是它到底是什麼樹呢？
這棵大樹竟然是小小的芥菜種所長成的芥菜樹啊！

"Oh my! Look!
This tree is taller than me!"
The tall corn shouted.
"Wow! The tree is bearing a lot of fruit too!"
All the tall trees were so jealous.

Guess what?
The big tree was the mustard tree who used to be a very small mustard seed!

「隔牆有耳！隔籬有眼！爸爸，這些成語都好有趣喔！」

"Walls have ears, hedges have eyes. Daddy! I think the old proverbs are so much fun!"

「艾蜜莉！不論歲月如何流逝，這些古老的成語，仍適用於現代的世界，並且這些珍寶的價值不僅沒有改變，還一直在世界中閃耀著它們的光芒呢！」

"Emily, no matter how the world changes, the old proverbs still apply to our lives now. The value in them never changes. It glows and inspires people even now!"

新與舊
New and Old

耶穌說：「這一切的話你們都明白了嗎？」他們說：「我們明白了。」
祂說：「凡文士受教作天國的門徒，就像一個家主從他庫裡拿出新舊的東西來。」
（馬太福音13：51－52）

很久以前，有一個以色列的家族，他們擁有一個世代相傳的書卷。
這個書卷非常珍貴，因為它記載了許多的智慧和應許。
而這個家族也願意把書卷裡的智慧和應許與人分享，
所以許多願意聽從的人，也都從這書卷中獲得很多的幫助。

這家族中有一位父親也重新做了一個新的書卷，
寫下他人生的智慧之言，
然後連同先前的那個舊書卷一起傳承給兒子。

A long time ago, in an Israelite family, there was a scroll which was passed down generation after generation.
This scroll was very precious because of the wisdoms and promises in it.
The family was willing to share the wisdoms and promises with everyone.
So people who followed the wisdoms in the scroll also got much help out of it.

The father in the family also wrote a new scroll,
which was written with all the wise words that he had learned through life.
And with the old scroll, the father passed them down to his son.

許多年過去了，世代不斷地交替，這些書卷也一代又一代地流傳下去。
「哎！祖先為什麼要流傳這些沒用的書卷？我真搞不懂！」
這位兒子根本不屑去讀這些書卷，就隨隨便便地把它們扔進倉庫了。

After many years, the scrolls were still passed down generation after generation.
"Ah, why are they passing down these useless scrolls? I don't get it."
One son didn't even bother to take a look at what was written on the scrolls and put them in the storage.

突然有一天，一位國家的高官派人聯絡這個家族，
他想要拜訪他們，閱讀他們的祖傳書卷。
因為他遇到一個無法解決的問題，
而且聽說這些書卷裡有他想要的解答。

兒子急急忙忙地跑去找那些存放在倉庫的書卷。

One day, someone in a very high position of the nation
made a visit to the family to read the scrolls.
He had an unsolvable problem and he heard that the scroll
would provide him with a solution.

The son ran into his storage room to find the scrolls.

倉庫裡滿是灰塵。

「哎喲！如果那些書卷被老鼠啃壞了，那我該怎麼辦？」

咳咳咳！哈⋯⋯啾！過了好一會兒，終於在倉庫的最底層發現了那書卷。

有些部分的書卷被損毀了，還有些書卷到處都長了霉，

幸好書卷裡的文字還看得到。

「呼⋯⋯呼！還好！還好！書卷看起來沒什麼問題。」

The storage room was full of dust.
"Oh no! What do I do if the rats nibbled parts of it away?"
Cough-cough! Ah-choo! It took him a while to finally find the scrolls
in the deepest part of the storage room.
Some parts of them were ruined
and mold was growing here and there.
Thankfully, the writings were fine.
"Phew. Okay, Okay.
Everything's okay."

37

「唉！我真是目光短淺，竟然小看了這麼珍貴的書卷！」
兒子終於了解到這些書卷所寫下的智慧和應許是多麼地有價值呀！
現在他正努力閱讀新書卷和舊書卷，
要把這些智慧和應許拿來教導人們。

"Oh, how short-sighted that I was to be little these precious scrolls!"
The son finally realized how valuable the written wisdoms and promises were!
Now he works hard on reading the new and the old scrolls
so as to share them with other people.

大衛非常後悔。

媽媽出門前曾交待他要好好照顧弟弟。
但是朋友們叫他一起去打棒球，他就跑出去玩了。
打完棒球後，他很擔心，因為他可以想像到媽媽對他生氣的表情。

然而因為他的真心悔改，媽媽就原諒他了。

David felt so regretful.

Mom had told him to take care of his younger brother while she went out.
But later, his friends came over and asked him to play baseball with them, so he went out to play.
After the game, he got worried because he could picture his mom being angry at him.

But seeing him honestly feeling sorry for what he had done, his mom forgave him.

兩個兒子
Two Sons

「你們再聽一個比喻;有個家主栽了一個葡萄園,周圍圈上籬笆,裡面挖了一個壓酒池,蓋了一座樓,租給園戶,就往外國去了。
收果子的時候近了,就打發僕人到園戶那裡去收果子。
園戶拿住僕人,打了一個,殺了一個,用石頭打死一個。
主人又打發別的僕人去,比先前更多;園戶還是照樣待他們。
後來打發他的兒子到他們那裡去,意思說:『他們必尊敬我的兒子。』
不料,園戶看見他兒子,就彼此說:『這是承受產業的。來吧,我們殺他,佔他的產業!』
他們就拿住他,推出葡萄園外,殺了。
園主來的時候要怎樣處治這些園戶呢?」
他們說:「要下毒手除滅那些惡人,將葡萄園另租給那按著時候交果子的園戶。」
(馬太福音21:33-41)

種植葡萄園的父親叫大兒子說：
「兒子，來，跟我一起去葡萄園工作。」
「好的，父親！」
父親也叫了他的小兒子。
「兒子啊，來，一起到葡萄園，幫爸爸做一些事！」
「我不要！我很忙！」
小兒子轉身掉頭就走了。

The father who takes care of a vineyard called out for his older son.
"Son, come and help me with the work in the vineyard."
"Okay, father!"
And the father also called his younger son.
"Son, come out and help your father!"
"No, I'm busy!" said the younger son,
who turned away without hesitation.

一看到大太陽，就想到要在烈日下汗流浹背的工作，
大兒子也就不想去葡萄園工作了。
「嗯……讓我想想有什麼好藉口。
對了！我就說，我要照顧生病的小羊，
沒辦法去葡萄園工作吧！嘻嘻……」
大兒子吹著口哨，往清涼的溪谷去釣魚了。

Seeing the scorching sun, the older son didn't want to work
because he would be sweating.
"Hmm. Let me think of a good excuse.
Yes! I'm going to tell dad that I am busy looking after
a sick baby lamb, and won't be able to help. Hee-hee……"
The older son walked away to go fishing
by the river as he whistled.

小兒子和朋友們玩得正起勁。
「讓我們來玩『用石頭打葡萄』的遊戲吧！」
「好像很好玩哦！我先來扔吧！
哈哈！打中了！打中了！你們看到沒？」
大家爭先恐後地拿起石頭打葡萄。
結實纍纍的葡萄被打爛了，掉了滿地。葡萄園也變得一片狼籍。

The younger son was having fun with his friends.
"Let's see who hits the most grapes with stones!"
"It sounds fun! Let me go first!
Yay! I got it! I got it! Did you see it?"
They all started to throw stones at the grapes.
The well-grown grapes were popped open
by the stones and fell all over the ground.
The vineyard was a mess.

47

「臭小子們！你們在幹什麼呀？」
大家聽到咆哮聲，就一溜煙地跑了。
「這些可惡的傢伙！你們知道我花了多少心血嗎？」
主人看著一片混亂的葡萄園，
卻哭不出來，
只能雙腳無力地癱坐在地上。

"Hey! Kids! What are you guys doing?"
Hearing the owner's shouting everyone ran away.
"Bad kids! Do you have any idea
how much effort I put in these grapes?"
Looking at the ruined vineyard,
the owner plunked down on the ground,
he had no tears left to cry.

躲在一旁觀看的小兒子，嚇呆了說：
「天呀！那……那是我爸爸的葡萄園！」
小兒子的父親正是那片葡萄園的主人。

The younger son who was hiding and watching
was so shocked that he couldn't move.
"That's… That's my father's…vineyard!"
It turned out that the owner
of the vineyard was his father.

49

小兒子心裡非常難過並且後悔地哭了起來。
「爸爸，真的對不起！對不起！」
父親用粗糙又溫暖的手，
摸摸低著頭、等著被教訓的小兒子，說：
「沒關係，兒子！雖然我很難過，但我還是很愛你的！」
從那時候起，小兒子成了父親最可靠的工作伙伴。

The younger son cried and regretted what he had done.
"Father, I'm sorry! I'm really sorry!"
The father used his rough but warm hand to pat the younger son,
who thought that he would be yelled at.
"That's okay, son. I am sad, but I still love you!"
From that day on, the younger son became the biggest help in the vineyard.

大衛在百貨公司裡和媽媽走失了。
他到處跑來跑去地找媽媽，
後來突然想到了一個好辦法。
他停下來，走向其中一個店員。

「嗚……嗚，我的媽媽不見了！請幫我找媽媽！」

沒多久，大衛就平安回到媽媽的懷抱。
店員稱讚大衛是一個聰明的小男孩。

David and his mom were at a shopping mall, but he got lost.
He was running to search for his mom,
but suddenly he came up with a good idea.
He stopped and went up to one of the workers.

"Sniff, sniffle. I lost my mommy! Please help me find my mom."

Later, he was safely in his mommy's arms.
The worker there praised David for being a smart boy.

所羅門王的智慧
Wisdom of King Solomon

一個說：「我主啊，我和這婦人同住一房；她在房中的時候，我生了一個男孩。
我生孩子後第三日，這婦人也生了孩子。我們是同住的，除了我們二人之外，房中再沒有別人。
夜間，這婦人睡著的時候，壓死了她的孩子。
她半夜起來，趁我睡著，從我旁邊把我的孩子抱去，放在她懷裡，將她的死孩子放在我懷裡。
天要亮的時候，我起來要給我的孩子吃奶，不料，孩子死了；及至天亮，我細細地察看，不是我所生的孩子。」
那婦人說：「不然，活孩子是我的，死孩子是你的。」這婦人說：「不然，死孩子是你的，活孩子是我的。」她們在王面前如此爭論。
王說：「這婦人說『活孩子是我的，死孩子是你的』，那婦人說『不然，死孩子是你的，活孩子是我的』」，
就吩咐說：「拿刀來！」人就拿刀來。王說：「將活孩子劈成兩半，一半給那婦人，一半給這婦人。」
活孩子的母親為自己的孩子心裡急痛，就說：「求我主將活孩子給那婦人吧，萬不可殺他！」
那婦人說：「這孩子也不歸我，也不歸你，把他劈了吧！」王說：「將活孩子給這婦人，萬不可殺他；這婦人實在是他的母親。」
以色列眾人聽見王這樣判斷，就都敬畏他；因為見他心裡有上帝的智慧，能以斷案。

（列王紀上3：17－28）

所羅門在很年輕的時候就當了國王。
「上帝啊！我很害怕治理整個國家。」

然後，上帝在他的夢中出現問他說：
「你要我給你什麼呢？」

「上帝啊！請賜給我智慧和知識！」

上帝很開心所羅門一心尋求它們，
所以不只應許他，
還賜給他福氣和榮耀。

Solomon became a king when he was really young.
"God! I have doubts if I am capable of ruling a kingdom."

Then God appeared in his dream and asked,
"What are you asking for from me?"

"God! Please give me wisdom and knowledge!"

God was happy that he asked only for wisdom and knowledge,
so God also promised Solomon
that He would give him blessing and glory.

有一天，有兩位婦人來到所羅門王的面前。
為了一個在她們面前的小孩而不停爭論著。

「我的國王呀！我早上起來一看，
那個女人竟然把她死掉的孩子偷偷地放在我的懷裡。
昨天晚上，她把自己的孩子壓死了，等我們都睡著後，
她就偷偷摸摸地把我的孩子和她的孩子調包了！」

「國王啊！她說謊！死了的孩子才是她的孩子，
這個活著的是我的！」

One day, two women came to King Solomon.
They were fighting over a baby.

"Oh my king, when I woke up in the morning,
the dead baby of that woman was in my arms.
Last night, that woman killed her baby by rolling over him, and while we were all asleep,
she secretly exchanged the dead baby with mine!"

"My king, she's lying! The dead baby is hers
and this living baby is mine."

所羅門王靜靜地聽完事情的來龍去脈，就下令說：
「來人啊！把刀拿來！
為了公平起見，把孩子劈成兩半吧！」
馬上就有其中一個女人號啕大哭地說：
「不可以這樣做！國王，請留下孩子的性命吧！
我願意把孩子讓給那個女人！」
但是另一個女人卻冷酷地說：
「不用了！國王，就如您所說的，為了公平起見，
就讓我和那女人都不能帶走孩子吧！」

After listening to everything carefully, King Solomon commanded,
"Bring a sword! Let's be fair and divide this baby into half
and give half to each woman."
Right at that moment, one of the women cried, saying,
"No, my king. Please don't hurt the baby.
I will let that woman have my baby!"
While the other woman said,
"No. Let's be fair and let
neither of us have the baby."

59

所羅門王露出會心一笑。

「那個想要救活孩子的女人，才是孩子真正的母親！

來人啊！把孩子交給她。」

那位真正的母親開心地抱著孩子回家了。

百姓們對所羅門王的智慧和判斷都讚嘆不已。

Then King Solomon smiled gladly.

"The woman who wants to save the baby is the real mother.

Servant, give the baby to her."

The real mom returned home happily with her baby.

People were impressed by the wisdom and judgment of King Solomon.

從此，所羅門王的睿智聲名遠播，傳遍整個世界。
各地的君王帶著金銀財寶來見所羅門王，為了要學習他的智慧。
向上帝尋求智慧的所羅門王；後來成為了一個偉大的國王。

From then on, King Solomon's reputation and wisdom spread throughout the world.
Kings from other empires visited King Solomon with gold and silver in exchange for his wisdom.
King Solomon, who had asked for wisdom from God, became a great king.

「大衛！你喜歡打棒球嗎？」
媽媽笑著問。

"David, do you like playing baseball?"
asked mom, smiling.

「媽咪，
雖然剛開始爸爸教我時，
我會很害怕，
但現在已經不會了！」

"Mommy, it was scary
when dad first taught me,
but it's okay now."

「以前，當我害怕球時，
爸爸就會緊緊地抓住我的手。」

"Dad used to hold my hands tight
when I was scared of the ball."

酵母
Yeast

祂又對他們講個比喻說：「天國好像麵酵，有婦人拿來，藏在三斗麵裡，直等全團都發起來。」
又說：「我拿什麼來比上帝的國呢？好比麵酵，有婦人拿來藏在三斗麵裡，直等全團都發起來。」
（馬太福音13：33；路加福音13：20－21）

現在剛做好的麵糰亂成一團。

發黃的老麵糰大聲吹牛說：
「你知道我以前是多麼有名嗎？
甚至太陽先生都會過來跟我握手！
我就是因為被太陽先生炙熱的手握過之後，
才會被燒得有點發黃了！」

The newly made dough was a mess.

The old dough which had become yellow bragged,
"I used to be really famous when I was young.
Even Mr. Sun came over to shake hands with me!
The sun was so hot that it gave me a tan.
That's why I'm yellow."

死腦筋的全麥麵糰非常膽戰心驚、深怕被脫了殼地說：
「健康的麵糰應該像我一樣，身上有著棕色的小殼。
像你這樣完全脫殼的白麵糰，是一點營養成分也沒有的！」

The stubborn whole-wheat dough, who was always afraid of losing its skin said,
"The healthy dough should have brown skin like me.
That white naked dough like you doesn't have any nutrients!"

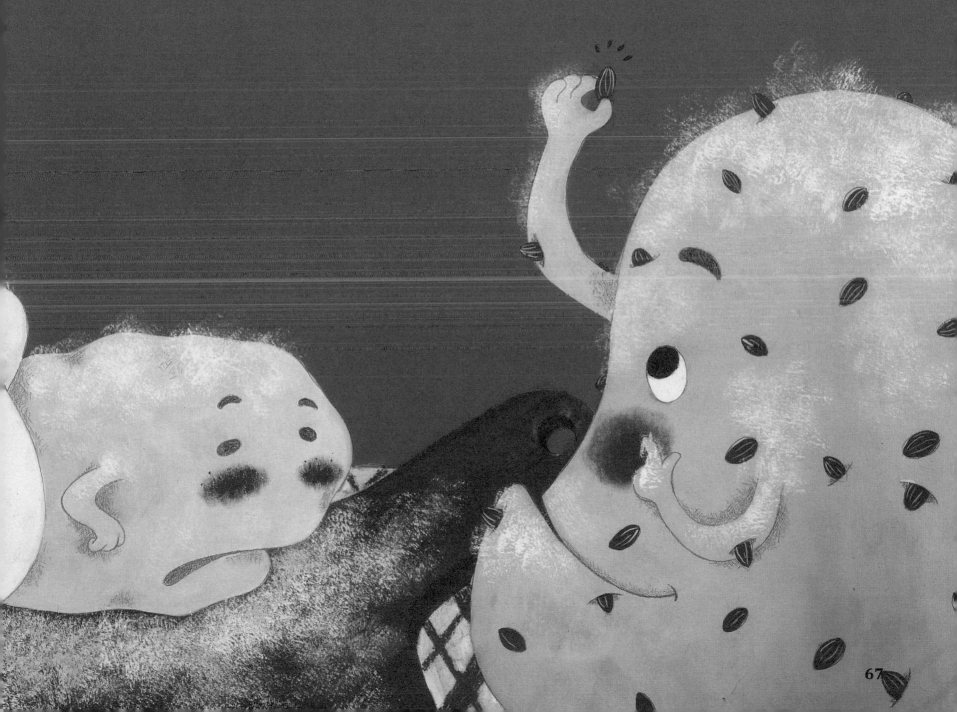

67

於是白麵糰不屑地說：
「哎喲！那個死腦筋的全麥麵糰可能是嫉妒又羨慕我雪白的臉蛋吧？」
結果，所有的麵糰們都因白麵糰有公主病而排擠它。

Then the white dough said with disdain,
"Urgh! Are you jealous of my white and clean skin, Mr. Stubborn?"
As a result, Everyone edged her out because she was such a spoiled princess.

一旁的醜八怪麵糰則是蜷曲成一團，喃喃自語地說：
「這世界上沒有像我一樣醜的麵糰了！有誰會願意做我的朋友呢？」

The ugly dough crouched and said to himself,
"No dough is as ugly as me. Who is willing to be my friend?"

69

所有的麵糰都有一個變成美味麵包的夢想。

「想要成為麵包，就必須要能膨脹！但到底該如何才能膨脹起來呢？」

「我不知道……，話是沒錯，但我怎麼試，就是不成功！」

All of the dough had one dream—to become delicious bread.

"To become bread, we have to puff up, but what do we have to do to puff up?"

"I don't know…I've been trying so hard. But it's not working at all!"

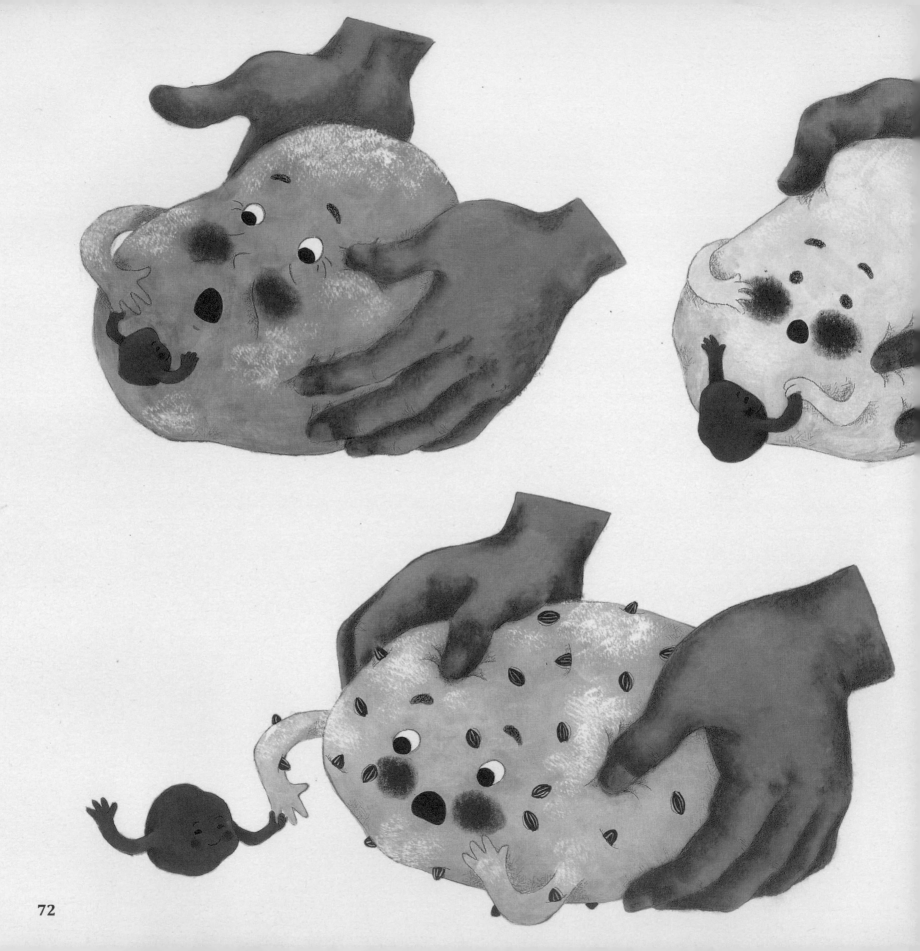

就在那時候，突然有人緊緊抓著他們的手，輕聲地說：

「吹牛大王，你變老並不是你的錯！」
「死腦筋，沒什麼好害怕的！就算沒有了麵皮，你仍然是很棒的。」
「公主病小姐，孤單嗎？我會一直在妳身邊的。」
「醜八怪，你知道你很迷人嗎？你的眼睛就像天上閃亮的星星！」
是誰在說話？原來是個子非常……非常小的酵母。

「我愛你們大家！」

Right at that moment, someone held their hands and said,

"Mr. Bluffer, it's not your fault that you are old."
"Mr. Stubborn, you don't have to be scared. You are good even without the skin."
"Miss Little Princess. Are you feeling lonely? I will always be with you."
"Mr. Ugly, do you know you're very charming? Your eyes are like stars in the sky!"
Who is talking? It was the tiny……little yeast.

"I love everyone of you!"

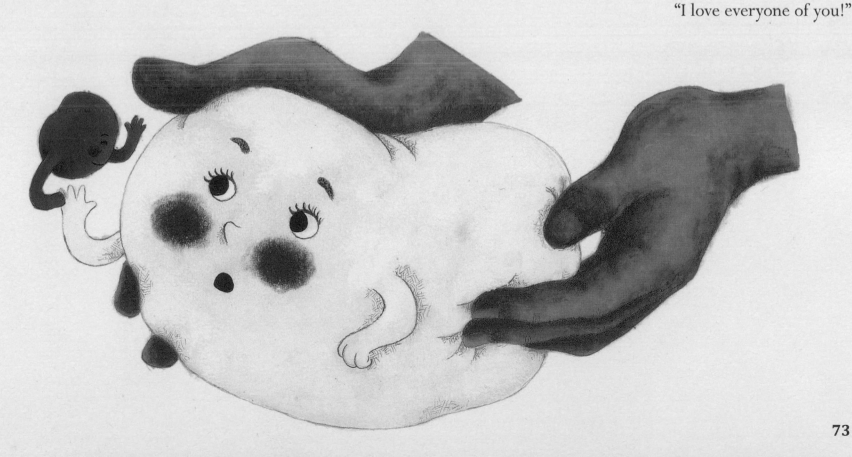

真是奇妙！突然好像發生了什麼事！
當他們遇見了酵母後，全身都變得暖暖的。
還有一股甜甜的香氣飄了出來！
那是麵糰感到幸福的時候，身上就會飄出的香氣。

啵啵啵……有氣泡從麵糰裡跑出來了……
那是麵糰呵呵笑的氣泡！

Amazing! It's like something marvelous just happened!
When they meet the yeast, their bodies start to warm up.
And they can smell sweetness from themselves.
It was the smell that is produced when dough is happy.

Then, air bubbles appeared…
It was the bubbles giggling out of the dough!

「哇！我們是什麼時候變成這個模樣的？」
像拳頭般大小的麵糰，在不知不覺之間變得像滿月般一樣圓潤飽滿。
「全都是託你的福，小酵母，謝謝你了！」

因為酵母的幫助，每個麵糰都能變成他們夢想中好吃的麵包了。

"Wow, when did we become like this?"
The dough that was once the size of a fist became full like a moon!
"It's all because of you. Thank you, little yeast!"

With help from the yeast,
each dough could become delicious bread
that they once dreamed of.

75

叮噹！叮噹！

大衛：哇！我的撲滿已經滿了！

媽媽：大衛現在是有錢人耶！你打算怎麼用這筆錢呢？

大衛：我想買想吃的東西，還想買玩具……。
　　　　嗯……既然這是我的錢，所以我想買什麼，就買什麼！

媽媽：好的。但在你買東西之前，
　　　　媽媽要跟你說一個有錢人的故事！

Chang-chang-chang!

David: Wow! My piggy bank is full!

Mommy: You are so rich now, David! What are you planning to do with it?

David: I'm going to get what I want to eat, my toys, and…
　　　　Well, the money is mine so I'm going to spend it as I like it!

Mommy: Okay, but before that,
　　　　let me tell you a story about a rich man.

愚昧的富人
The Foolish Rich Man

就用比喻對他們說：「有一個財主田產豐盛；
自己心裡思想說：『我的出產沒有地方收藏，怎麼辦呢？』
又說：『我要這麼辦：要把我的倉房拆了，另蓋更大的，在那裡好收藏我一切的糧食和財物，
然後要對我的靈魂說：靈魂哪，你有許多財物積存，可作多年的費用，只管安安逸逸地吃喝快樂吧！』
上帝卻對他說：『無知的人哪，今夜必要你的靈魂；你所預備的要歸誰呢？』
凡為自己積財，在上帝面前卻不富足的，也是這樣。」

（路加福音12：16－21）

「哇！今年真是大豐收！大豐收啊！好！哈哈哈！」
在這個富人的院子裡，放著堆積如山、一袋又一袋的穀物，
因為他的倉庫都已經放滿了。

但是並不是每個人都有很好的收成。

"**Wow!** What a bumper harvest this year! Very nice! Ha-ha-ha!"
The rich man's yard was filled with mountains of crops
because his storage house was already full.

But not everybody had a plentiful harvest.

「主人！既然今年你有多餘的糧食，何不借給拉撒路一點呢？
他失去了父母和爺爺，現在和奶奶住在一起。
他們都餓到不行了，生活又非常困難，還有……」
「好了！好了！不用再講了！
那些乞丐又沒做什麼事，為什麼我要把我的糧食分給他們？
這件事就別再提了！去做你自己的事吧！」
「……」

"Sir, since there are abundant crops this year,
why don't you let Lazarus have some of them?
He had lost his grandfather and parents
and now lives with his grandmother.
They are suffering from hunger.
Their life is difficult, and……"
"No! Stop it!
Those beggars didn't do anything for me.
Why do I have to share my crops with them?
Don't ever ask me for that kind of favor again.
Mind your own business."
"……"

「現在就把那個倉庫拆了！」
「什麼？主人，我還要再蓋一個倉庫，一個比現在更大的倉庫！」
富人指揮著他的僕人如何去建造一個新的倉庫。
很快地，一個又大又新的倉庫完工了。

"Now, take that storage down",
"What? Master, I'm going to build another one, a much bigger one!"
The rich man ordered his servants to build a new storage house.
And soon after, a big new storage house was built.

沒多久，新的大倉庫裡也裝了滿滿的糧食。
「哈哈哈！之後的幾年都不用擔心沒東西吃了！
我現在可以高枕無憂地吃喝玩樂了！」

Before long, the new storage house was full of crops, too.
"Ha-ha-ha! I don't have to worry about food for the next couple of years!
I can just have fun all day and night!"

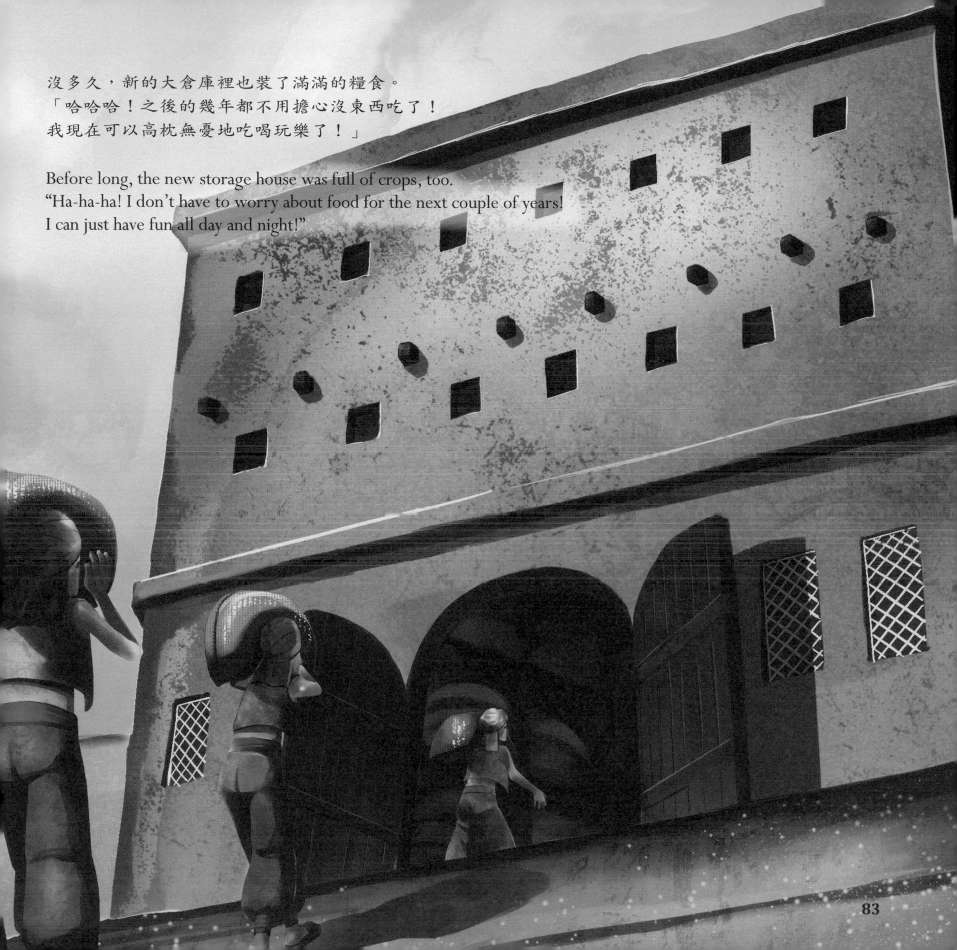

那天晚上，他夢到上帝對他說：
「我賜福給你的理由，是希望你能夠去幫助那些有困難的人們，
但是你很自私，只顧著自己的貪念而已。
今晚我若取了你的性命，
那倉庫裡所積存的一切要歸給誰呢？
你這愚蠢的人啊！」

That night in his dream, God said,
"One of the reasons why I blessed you is to have you share it with those in need,
but you are so selfish and greedy. You care only about yourself.
Why didn't you realize that everything you saved
for yourself will become useless
if I take your life tonight? You foolish man!"

在那天晚上，富人就死了！

And that night, God took his life!

在倉庫裡積存滿滿的糧食，現在也一無用處了，
因為就算有堆積如山的財寶，也不能買到生命。

The abundant crops in the storage house seemed useless,
because all the riches in this world cannot make a person live longer.

「哎呀！你把我的消防車弄壞了啦！」
大衛很生氣的打了朋友。

「嗚哇……嗚哇！」

朋友一邊哭一邊跑走了。
大衛一整天都心情不好。

「我要不要原諒他呢？」

"Hey! You broke my fire truck!"
David beat his friend angrily.

"Waaaah--"

His friend walked away crying loudly.
David felt bad all day.

"Should I forgive him?"

饒恕
Forgiveness

天國好像一個王要和他僕人算帳。
才算的時候，有人帶了一個欠一千萬銀子的來。
因為他沒有什麼償還之物，主人吩咐把他和他妻子兒女，並一切所有的都賣了償還。
那僕人就俯伏拜他，說：『主啊，寬容我，將來我都要還清。』
那僕人的主人就動了慈心，把他釋放了，並且免了他的債。
「那僕人出來，遇見他的一個同伴欠他十兩銀子，便揪著他，掐住他的喉嚨，說：『你把所欠的還我！』
他的同伴就俯伏央求他，說：『寬容我吧，將來我必還清。』
他不肯，竟去把他下在監裡，等他還了所欠的債。
眾同伴看見他所做的事就甚憂愁，去把這事都告訴了主人。
於是主人叫了他來，對他說：『你這惡奴才！你央求我，我就把你所欠的都免了，
你不應當憐恤你的同伴，像我憐恤你嗎？』
主人就大怒，把他交給掌刑的，等他還清了所欠的債。
你們各人若不從心裡饒恕你的弟兄，我天父也要這樣待你們了。」
（馬太福音18：23－35）

在王宮裡工作的一個僕人被帶到國王面前。
國王非常嚴厲地質問他：
「我叫你負責管理王宮的財務，你竟然浪費了所有的錢，
甚至還欠了一萬個他連得☀！」
「我錯了！請原諒我！
我會還給您的。」僕人不停抖動著身體。

90

A servant who worked in the palace was brought to the King.
The King snarled at him, asking,
"I commanded you to manage the finances, but how dare you to lose all the money
and even owe ten thousand talents?"
"Please forgive me! It's my fault.
I will pay you back," said the servant, shivering.

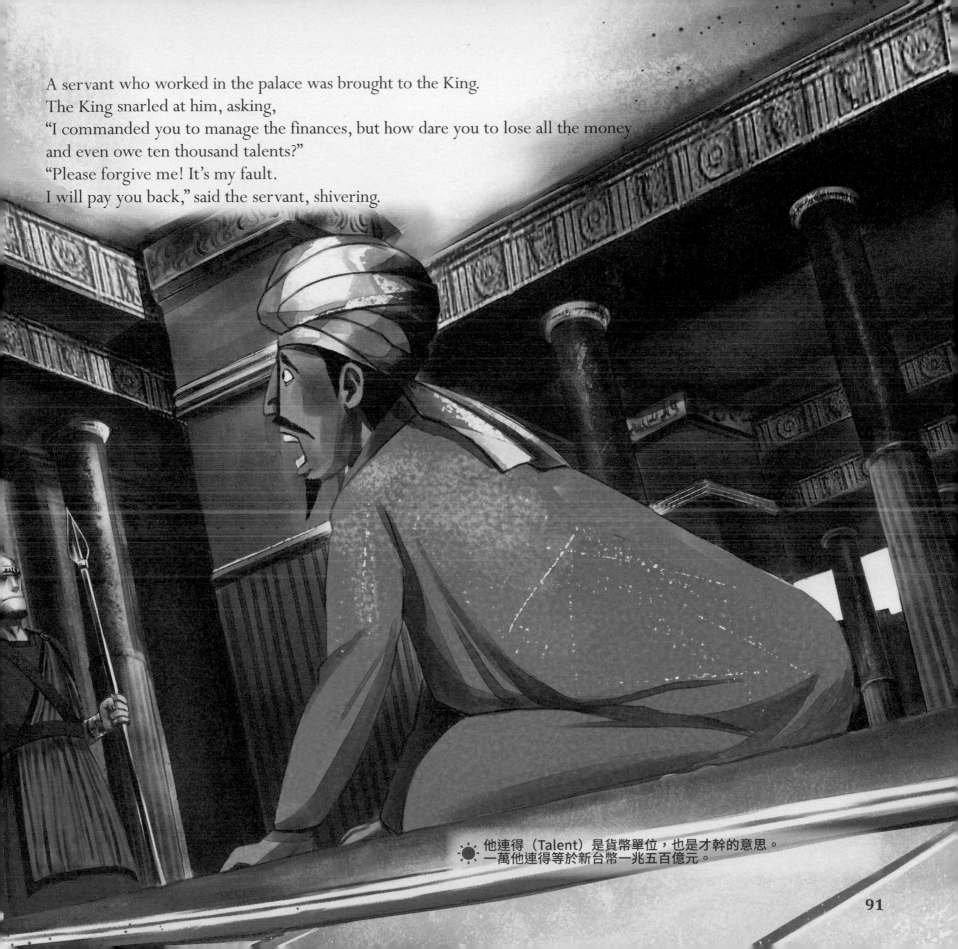

他連得（Talent）是貨幣單位，也是才幹的意思。
一萬他連得等於新台幣一兆五百億元。

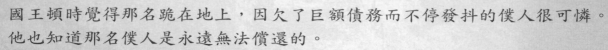

國王頓時覺得那名跪在地上，因欠了巨額債務而不停發抖的僕人很可憐。
他也知道那名僕人是永遠無法償還的。
「唉！你要用什麼償還這一萬他連得呢？
算了，我就一筆勾銷你所有的債務，以後好好地生活吧！」

The King suddenly took pity on the servant,
who was kneeling down shivering because of the huge debt.
He knew that it was impossible for the servant to pay him back.
"Ah! How are you going to pay ten thousand talents?
Forget it, I'll cancel your debt.
Just leave and make the best of your life!"

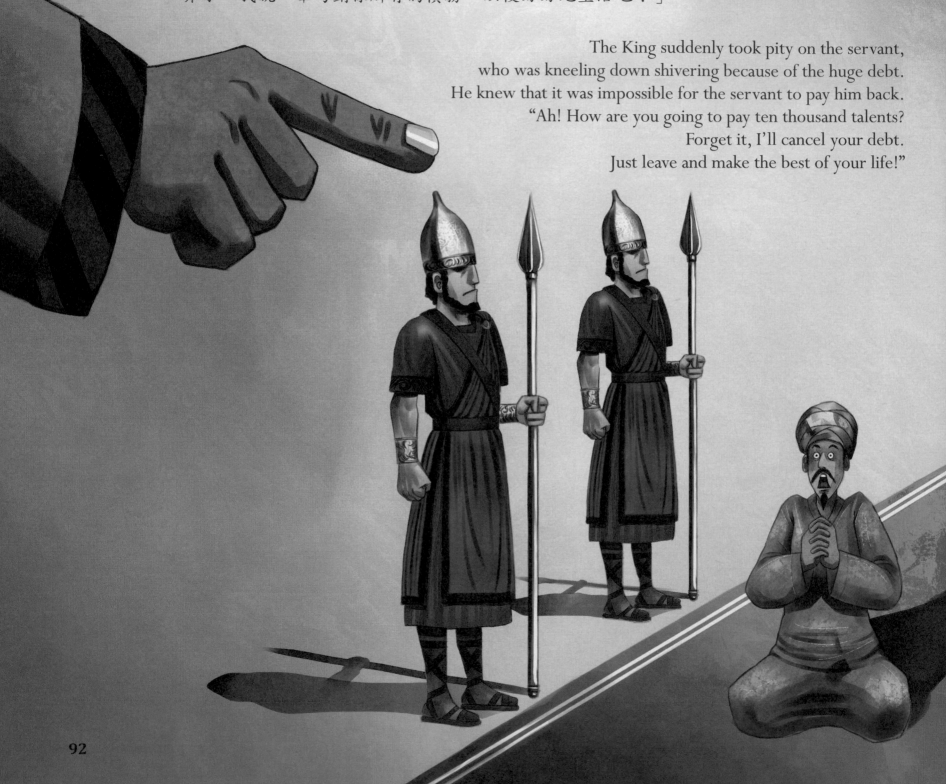

「唷！得救了！我是多麼地幸運啊！哈哈哈！」
慷慨的國王免除了那位僕人所有債務的風聲，
一下子在街頭巷尾傳為美談。

"Phew! I am so lucky! Ha-ha-ha!"
The news that the generous king had forgiven
the servant spread all over the streets.

被國王免了債的僕人，心情愉快地走在街上，
在街上遇見了欠他一百銀錢的朋友。
「嘿！就這麼巧，被我逮到了！」
他不分青紅皂白的，就抓住了朋友的領子。
「你欠我一百個銀錢，對吧？什麼時候要還啊？」
「對不起，我一定會還給你的，請再給我一點時間！」

「不行！現在！馬上就還給我！」

On the way back home, the servant who was forgiven walked happily.
He bumped into a friend who owed him a hundred denarii☀.
"Aha! There you are!" the servant grabbed him by the collar.
"You owe me a hundred denarii, don't you? When are you going to pay me back?"
"I'm sorry. Give me a little more time. I will pay you back for sure!"

"No! Pay me back right now!"

☀ 得拿利（denarii）是羅馬帝國的貨幣單位，即一銀錢的意思。
一他連得等於六千得拿利。

這個僕人毫不留情地拖著朋友進到監獄，說：
「除非你還清所有的欠款，否則就別想出來！」
The servant dragged him and put him in jail with no mercy.
"Don't even dream about getting out unless you pay me back!"

95

鎮上的人們開始對這個僕人的行為議論紛紛。
「太不公平了！他自己欠了那麼大的一筆錢，都不用還了！
但竟然對只欠一百個銀錢的朋友這樣做？」
「真是太可恥了！」

People in town started to whisper and gossip about the servant.
"It's unfair! He himself was spared with all that huge debt!
And now he does this to his friend who owe him only a hundred denarii?"
"Shame on him!"

聽到這件事的國王，再次抓了那個僕人。
「你這個惡人！我因為覺得你可憐，所以免去了你所有的債務。
但你做了什麼事？你竟然為了區區一百個銀錢，就把朋友關進了牢裡。
來人啊！把他關進監牢裡，
直到他還了我一萬個他連得為止，才可以放他出來！」

When the King heard about what happened, he arrested the servant again.
"You evil man! I felt pity on you so I forgave you.
But what did you do? You put your friend in jail for merely a hundred denarii!
Guards! Put this man in jail and don't let him out
until he repays me ten thousand talents!"

僕人忘了自己所受的恩惠而無情地對待朋友。
他自己用腳踢走了國王對他的憐憫和饒恕。

The servant showed no mercy to his friend, not knowing the grace he had received.
He tossed aside the mercy and forgiveness he got from the King.

有一位老奶奶用拖車載著許多廢紙，
步履蹣跚地走在山丘上。

大衛：媽媽，我們來幫助她好嗎？
大衛和媽媽一起幫老奶奶推車。
大衛：好怪喔！雖然喘得要命，但是我卻很開心。
媽媽：大衛，你今天算是老奶奶的好鄰居。

An old lady was shakily pushing a cart loaded with waste papers up a hill.

David: Mom, shall we go and help her?
Mom and David helped the old woman.
David: It's weird! It's very tiring, but I felt pretty good.
Mommy: David, you are a good neighbor for the old lady today.

善良的撒馬利亞人
The Good Samaritan

耶穌回答說：「有一個人從耶路撒冷下耶利哥去，落在強盜手中。他們剝去他的衣裳，把他打個半死，就丟下他走了。

偶然有一個祭司從這條路下來，看見他就從那邊過去了。

又有一個利未人來到這地方，看見他，也照樣從那邊過去了。

惟有一個撒馬利亞人行路來到那裡，看見他就動了慈心，

上前用油和酒倒在他的傷處，包裹好了，扶他騎上自己的牲口，帶到店裡去照應他。

第二天拿出二錢銀子來，交給店主，說：『你且照應他；此外所費用的，我回來必還你。』

你想，這三個人哪一個是落在強盜手中的鄰舍呢？」

他說：「是憐憫他的。」耶穌說：「你去照樣行吧！」

（路加福音10：30－37）

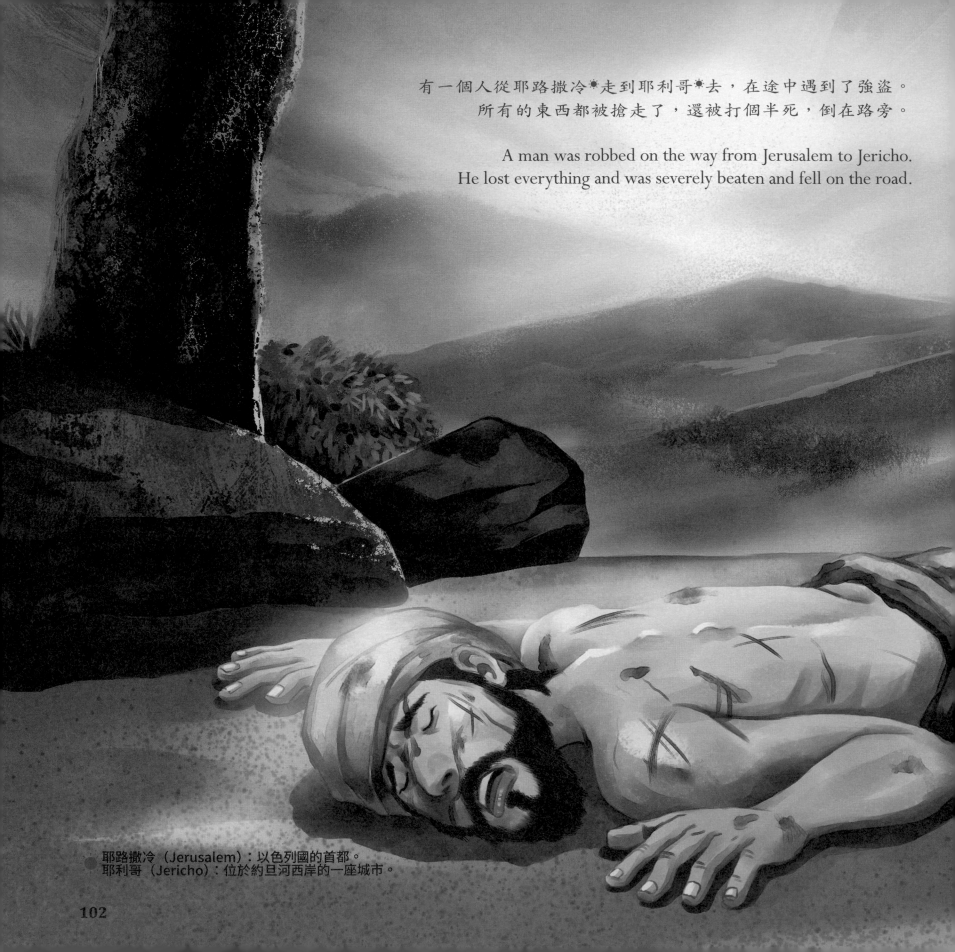

有一個人從耶路撒冷✹走到耶利哥✹去，在途中遇到了強盜。
所有的東西都被搶走了，還被打個半死，倒在路旁。

A man was robbed on the way from Jerusalem to Jericho.
He lost everything and was severely beaten and fell on the road.

耶路撒冷（Jerusalem）：以色列國的首都。
耶利哥（Jericho）：位於約旦河西岸的一座城市。

102

有一位剛參加完祭典的祭司長，
看到那被強盜打到渾身是血的人。
「哼！不潔淨！不潔淨！為什麼偏偏是我看見了？
現在連我的眼睛也不潔淨了！呸！」
祭司長遠遠地繞過去，急急忙忙地避開他。

A chief priest happened to pass by after a worship service
and saw the man covered in blood after being beaten by the robber.
"Ugh! How unclean he is! Why does he have to be there?
Now even my eyes are unclean. Bah!"
The chief priest took a detour to avoid the man immediately.

才沒過不久，又有一位利未人，
在同一條路上看到那個倒在路上的人。
「哦！看起來他急需要別人幫忙。
嗯！但這關我什麼事呢？
反正最後會有人來幫他的！」

A little bit later, a Levite was walking on the same road
and saw the same man lying on the road.
"Oh! he seems to need help desperately.
But why do I care so much?
Someone else will help him eventually."

利未人連忙走避，快步離開了。

The Levite walked away in a hurry, too.

傍晚時，有一個撒馬利亞人☀剛好也經過那條路。
「哇！嚇我一跳！這個人為什麼躺在這裡？
喔，我的天呀！看起來他遇到強盜了。不對！這個人快死了！
快沒有時間了！」
他毫不猶豫，馬上拿出葡萄酒倒在那人的傷口上消毒，再抹上油。
然後撕開自己的衣服，
將那人的傷口包紮好，帶到旅店。

In the evening, a Samaritan was also walking down the same road.
"Whoa! That scared me! Why is someone lying down here?
Oh my! It looks like someone has robbed him. He's dying!
There is no time to waste."
The Samaritan took out his wine
to sterilize the man's wounds and put oil on them.
Then he ripped off a piece of his own clothing
to wrap the wounds,
and then he took the man to an inn.

☀撒馬利亞人（Samaritan）：古代以色列分
裂成南國與北國，撒馬利亞是當時北國以
色列的首都，北國被亞述侵略而滅國後，
從亞述移民過來的人和以色列的人通婚後
而產生新的人種。南方的猶太人完全認為
撒馬利亞人的血統不純正，因而排斥他們。

隔天早晨，撒馬利亞人再次拜託旅店主人。
「我這裡有兩個銀錢，請好好照顧這個人！
錢若是不夠的話，等我回程的時候，再付你錢。」

The next morning, the Samaritan came to the inn and told the owner,
"Here are two denarii. Please take care of him.
If it's not enough, I'll pay you when I come back."

撒馬利人趕緊騎著驢子趕路去了。

「我得趕快把事情做完，再回來看看他！」

踢躂！踢躂！

The Samaritan hurried on his way.

"I've got to finish my work as soon as possible and come back to take care of that poor man."

Clip-clop, clip-clop…

請找出與左圖不同的地方：
★ 簡單10個
★★ 中級8個
★★★ 極難4個

113

前頁解答